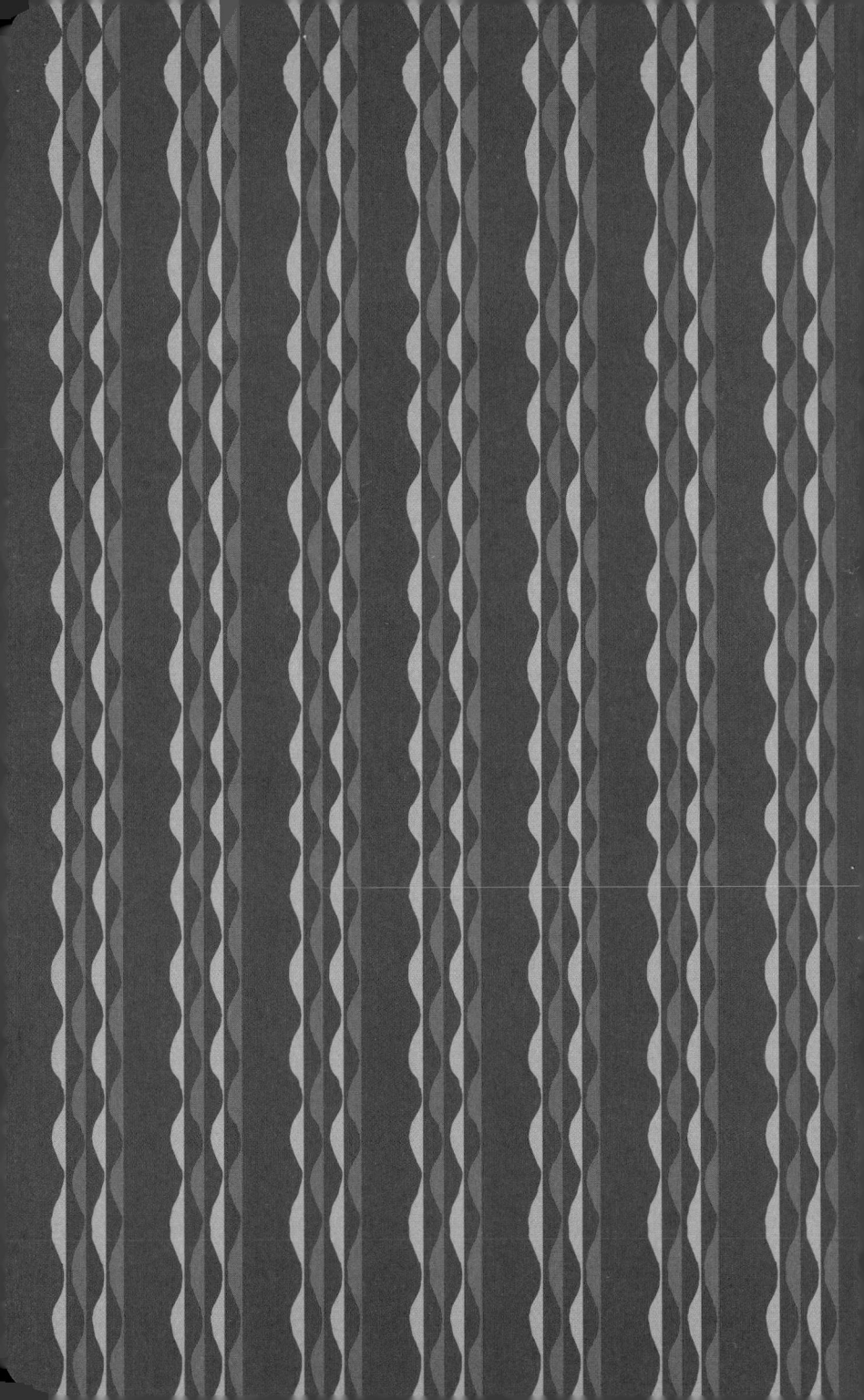

IT WAS A TIME WHEN THE

UNTHINKABLE

BECAME THE

THINKABLE

AND THE

IMPOSSIBLE

REALLY

HAPPENED.

- ARUNDHATI ROY

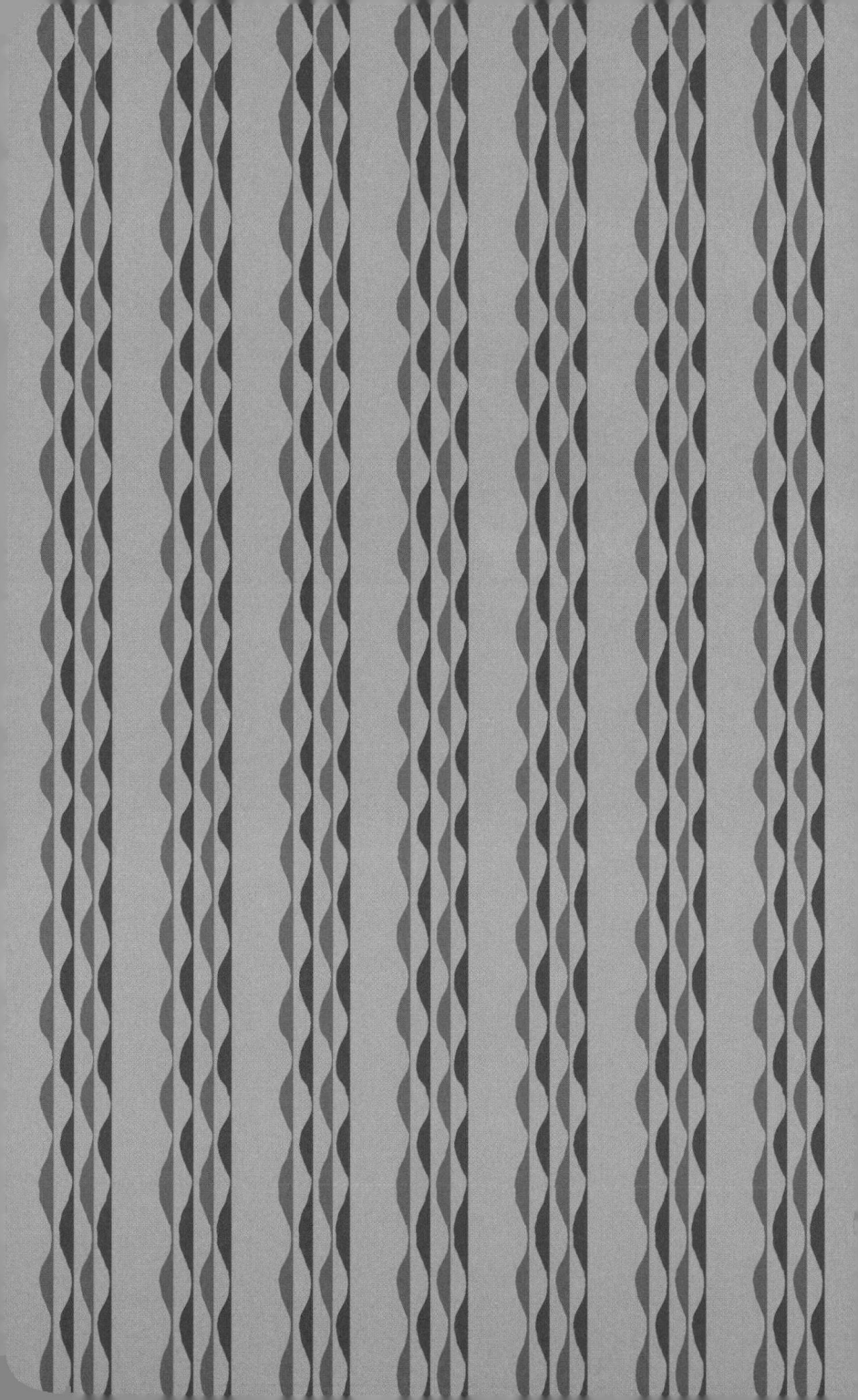

Never Lose

AN OPPORTUNITY OF SEEING

ANYTHING

THAT IS

Beautiful...

- RALPH WALDO EMERSON

Somewhere,
SOMETHING
INCREDIBLE
IS WAITING TO BE
KNOWN.
-CARL SAGAN

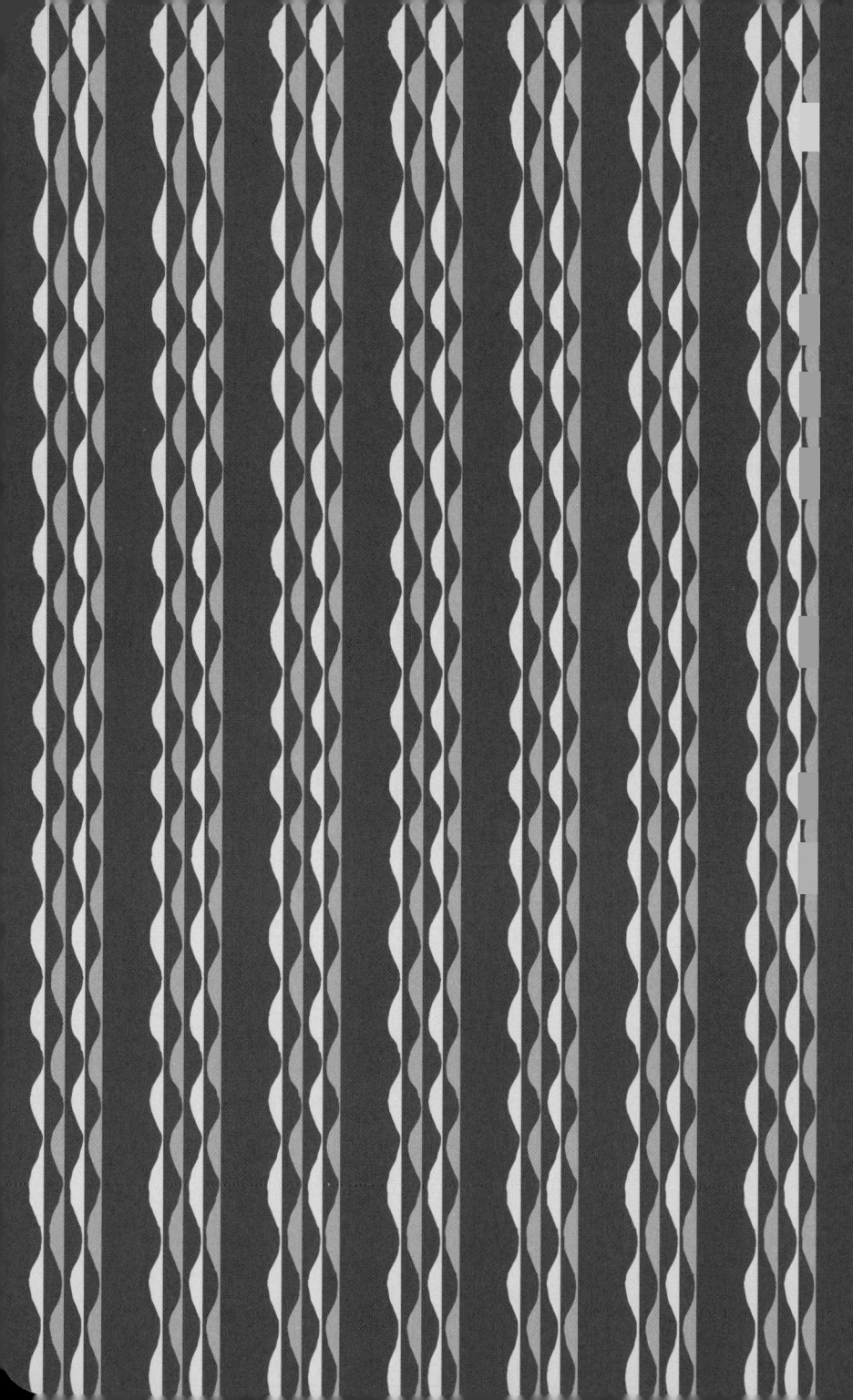

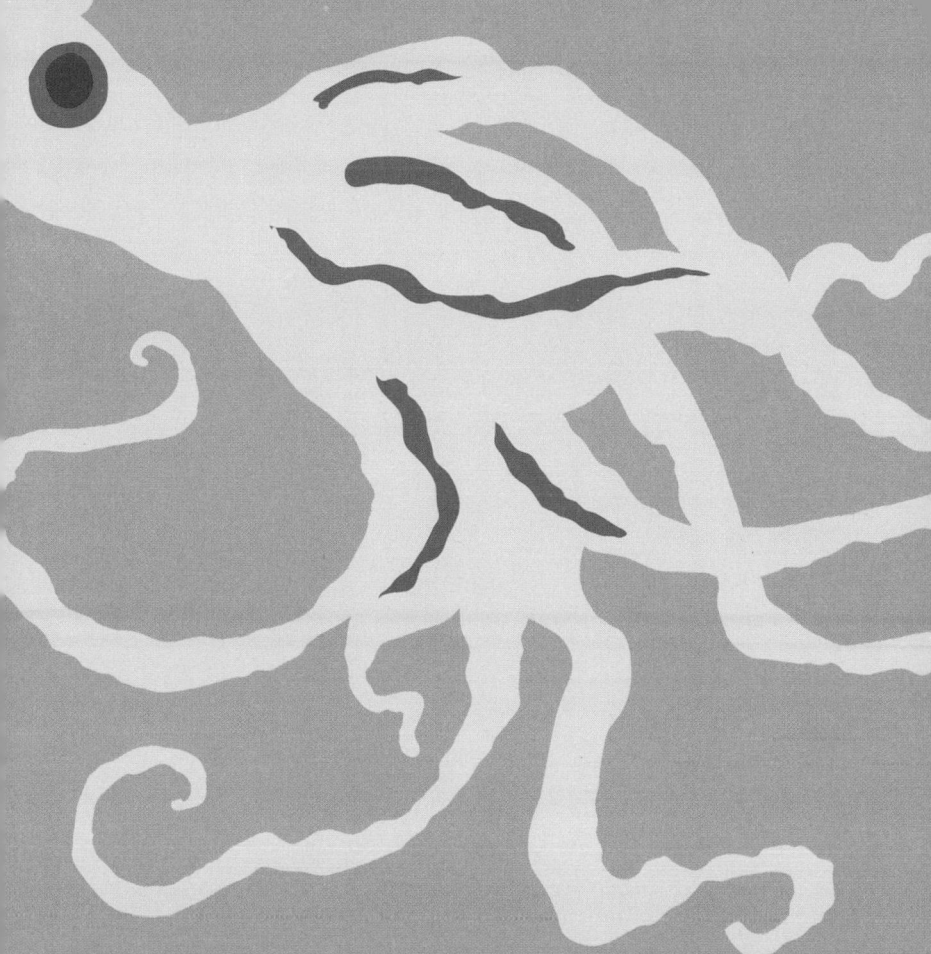

THERE ARE NO

BOUNDARIES

— ONLY

POSSIBILITIES.

— SAKYONG MIPHAM RINPOCHE

THE
Best Parts
OF THIS
WORLD
WERE NOT
Fashioned
BY THOSE WHO WERE
REALISTIC.

THEY WERE FASHIONED
BY THOSE WHO DARED TO
Look hard

AT THEIR WISHES
AND GAVE THEM
HORSES TO
RIDE.

- RICHARD BOLLES

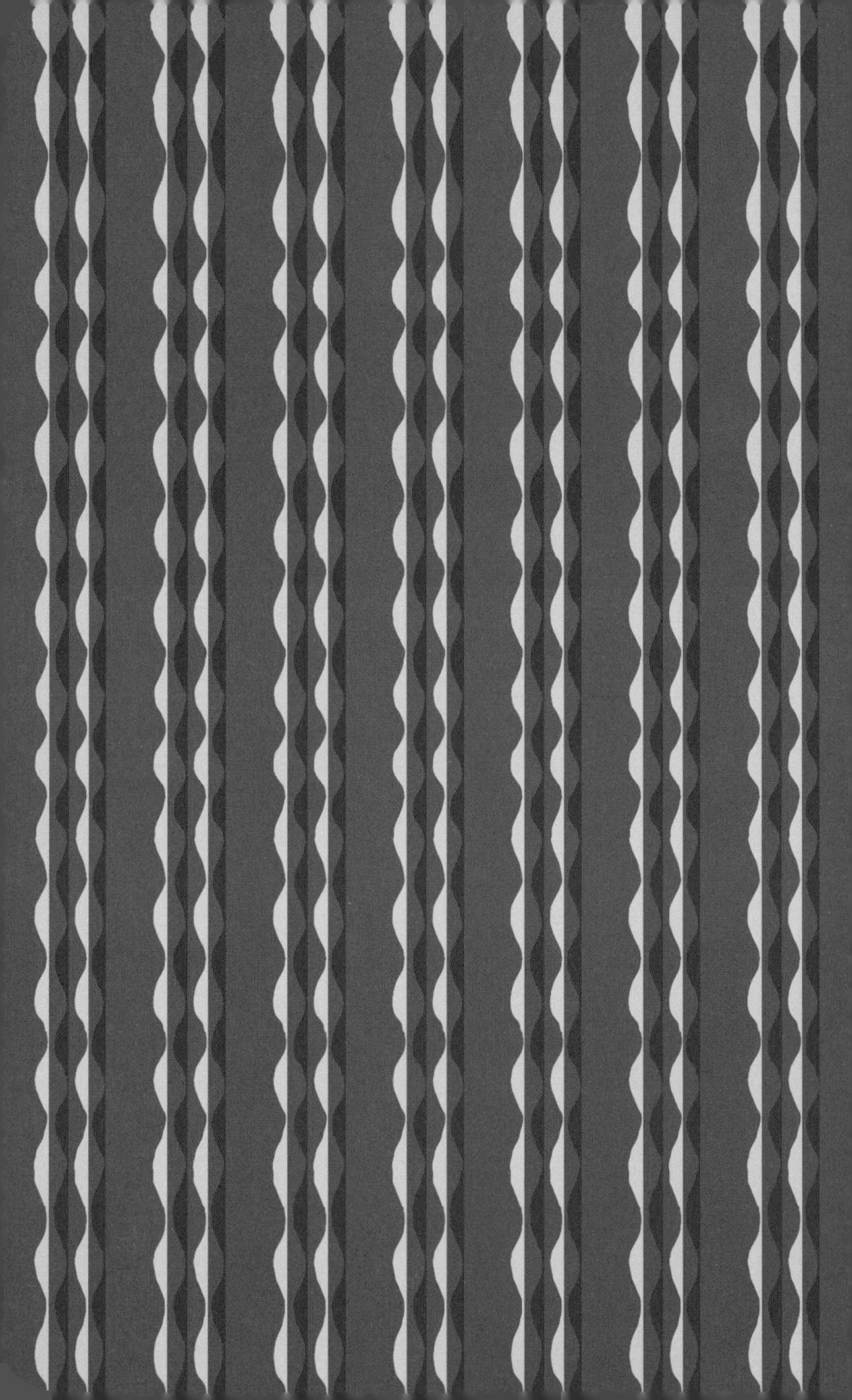

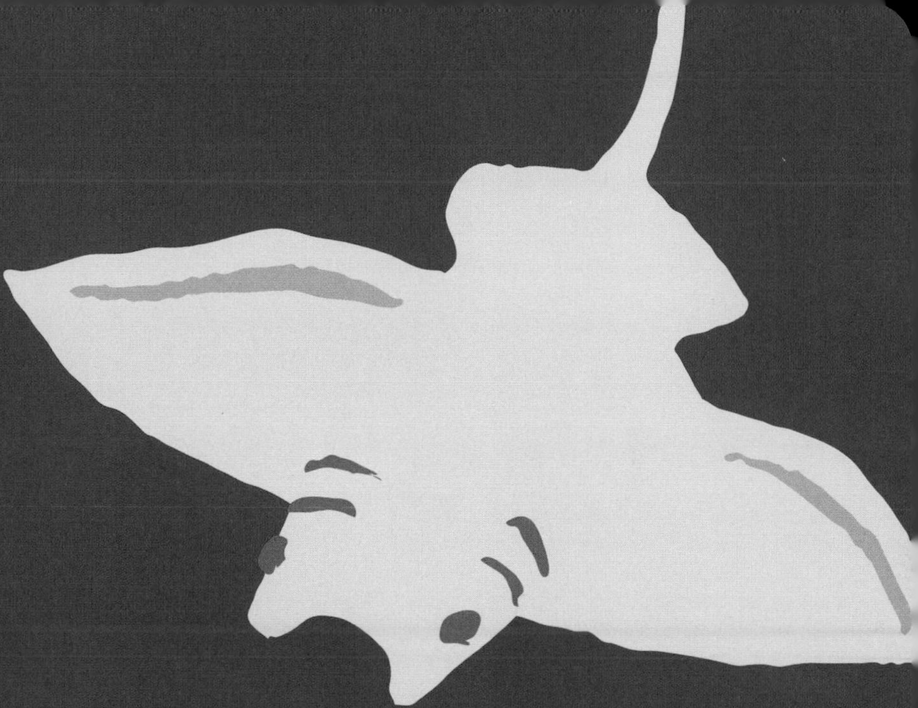

THE **SiMPLE THiNGS** ARE ALSO THE MOST **EXTRAORDINARY THINGS,** AND ONLY THE WISE CAN **See THEM.**

- PAULO COELHO

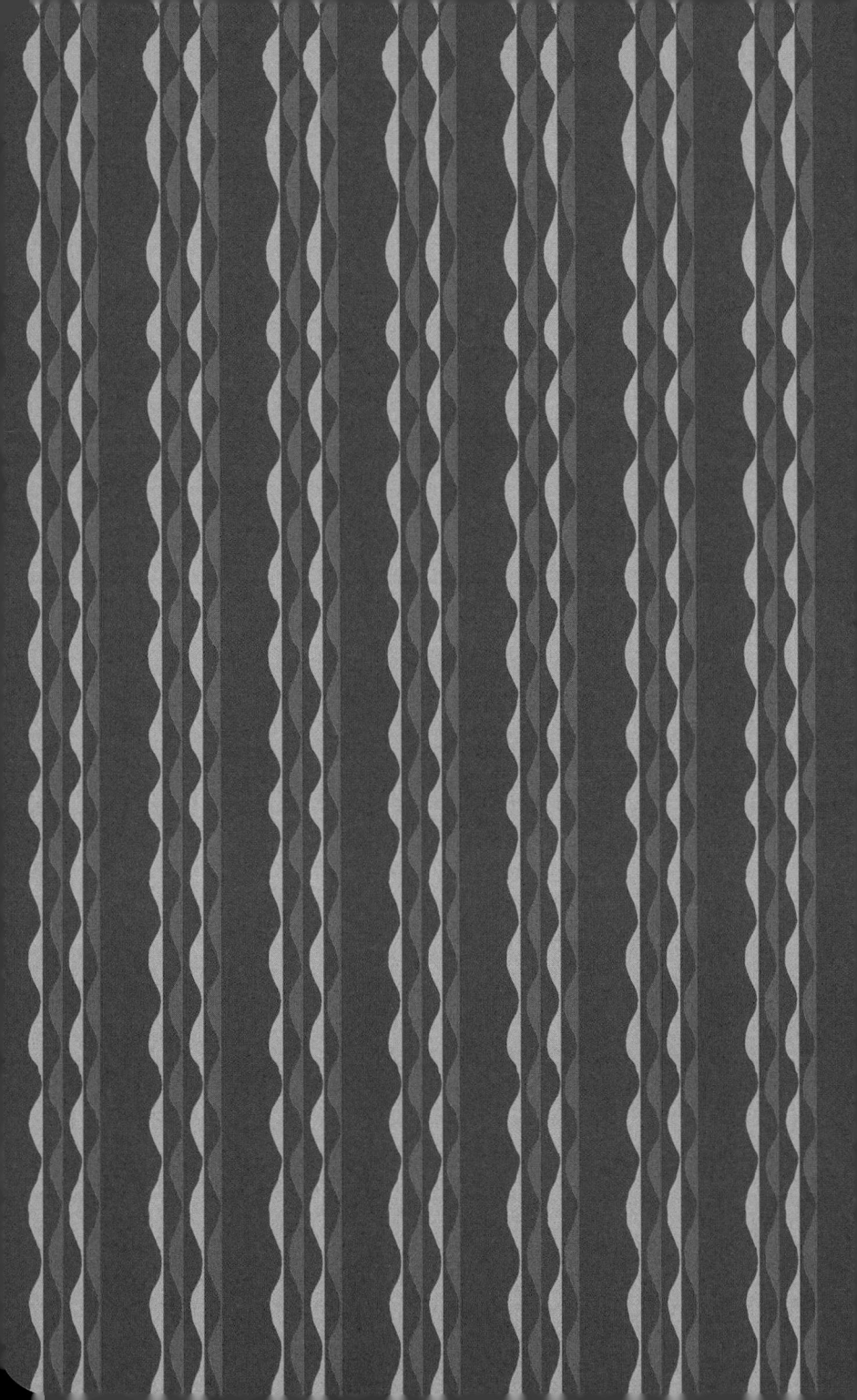

AS TO ME I KNOW OF

Nothing else

BUT

MIRACLES...

- WALT WHITMAN

WE WILL HAVE
MEANING

BEYOND

MEANING

& HAPPINESS

BEYOND

HAPPINESS...

-DARIN LANG